Silly Jack and the Beanstalk

Written by
Malachy Doyle

Illustrated by
Alexandra Colombo

Jack's mum was cross.
"We have no food left,"
she said.
"Jack, go and sell the cow!"

Jack sold the cow to a farmer.
The farmer gave him some beans.

“Silly Jack!” said Mum.
She threw the beans into the garden.

The next day, a **big**, **green** plant was growing in the garden.

"I will climb up to the top," said Silly Jack.

At the top, Jack saw a castle.
He went to it.
Hide, boy!
A giant lives here.
He will eat you!

Silly Jack hid.

"**I smell boy!**" said the giant.
"No, it is the stew,"
said the giant's wife.

The giant went in the castle.
"**Lay!**" he said to his hen.
The hen laid some golden eggs.

The giant went to sleep.
Jack took the hen and ran off.
He began to climb down the beanstalk.

The giant woke up ...
and saw him!
The giant came down
the beanstalk after Jack.

But Jack was too quick!

“Get me an axe, Mum!” he said.
He chopped and chopped at the beanstalk.
At last it fell to the ground.